Eric Vanderburg

Practical Considerations for Software Development

Der GRIN Verlag publiziert seit 1998 wissenschaftliche Arbeiten von Studenten, Hochschullehrern und anderen Akademikern als eBook und gedrucktes Buch. Die Verlagswebsite www.grin.com ist die ideale Plattform zur Veröffentlichung von Hausarbeiten, Abschlussarbeiten, wissenschaftlichen Aufsätzen, Dissertationen und Fachbüchern.

Document Nr. V205029

Eric Vanderburg

Practical Considerations for Software Development

GRIN Verlag

Die Deutsche Bibliothek verzeichnet diese Publikation in der Deutschen Nationalbibliografie; detaillierte bibliografische Daten sind im Internet über http://dnb.d-nb.de/ abrufbar.

1. Auflage 2011
Copyright © 2011 GRIN Verlag GmbH
http://www.grin.com
Druck und Bindung: Books on Demand GmbH, Norderstedt Germany
ISBN 978-3-656-34879-5

Practical Considerations for Software Development

Eric Vanderburg

Table of Contents

Table of Figures

Overview

This book provides a practical approach to developing software. It introduces a framework concerned with the planning, analysis, design, and implementation of software. The framework is concerned with the entire software development process starting from identifying the business need for software and ending with the finished deliverables.

Software Strategy

The goal is to deliver quality software to the client. The software project is planned, analyzed, and design to create a "blueprint" before coding is started. These are essential steps taken before the programmer starts implementation (coding) to ensure the programmer has specific requirements, obtainable goals, and a measurable workload.

Each phase has deliverable(s):

- Planning: Program specifications (requirements document)
- Analysis and Design: Class diagram (converts to skeleton code)
- Implementation: Program release

Planning

This section states the essential steps in the planning phase: the concept of the software (the business need), feasibility analysis and creating requirements. Planning starts with conceptualizing the idea and ends with requirements. The planning stage goal is a requirements document (program specification) to give to the programmer (or possibly software systems analyst).

Involvement level:

- Team members with high involvement: managers, stakeholders
- Team members with some involvement: developer

Planning starts with the software concept: either a team member or a stakeholder in the organization conceives an idea to fulfill a business need. This idea is generally a business solution for a problem. For example

- Business need: Organization XYZ wants to cut paper consumption
- Business solution: Create a software system that stores documents electronically to reduce paper consumption

Once the concept of a business solution is created, management must decide the feasibility of the project. This may consist of deciding if it is worth investing in the development of a software solution and whether it can be done. If the project is approved, the requirements document or program specification is created.

The program specification document is a requirements document that states the features and goals of the software. The document should contain an overview, key terms, scope, skeleton/demo (optional), milestones (goals), code review (testing plan), and project management information. The sections are as follows:

- Overview: the purpose of the program and the business need it solves
- Key terms: common words, technical terms, acronyms, etc. pertaining to the program specification document
- Scope: a very high level outline of the program features and specifications
- Skeleton/Demo (optional): screenshots or drawn forms of the user interface
- Milestones: The program goals. Use the scope section and select a several goals which will be obtained be either a version number or date

NOTE: It is possible for the Concept → Feasibility Analysis → Requirements steps to go through several iterations. For example, if the software concept is created, management may want a draft of program specifications too see if the project is feasible. MS Visio can be used to draw demo .NET forms to show a concept or a small skeleton program may be created to show the functionality.

Analysis and Design

This section describes the analysis and design phase of software development which integrates UML 2.0 to create a "blueprint" of the software system. The "blueprint" will be used by the programmer in the implementation phase to code the software. Each UML diagram and document is discussed in each subsection. The program specifications should contain enough information to start analysis and design. Five essential UML diagrams and documents are created in this process: activity diagram, use case descriptions, use case diagram, CRC cards, and class diagram. UML diagrams are drawn with CASE tools or general diagram drawing software (MS Visio). UML documents are templates created from a word processor.

The UML documents and diagrams are created by either a programmer or analyst familiar with UML. These created documents/diagrams are meant to help the technical staff develop the software. It is recommended the diagrams are reviewed by peers, but review under the discretion there is never a perfect diagram. Each diagram and document is a general explanation of each entity. The goal is diagrams have a logical flow and the documents have general detail.

Involvement level:

- Team members with high involvement: programmer or software systems analyst
- Team member with some involvement: managers, stakeholders

Activity Diagram

When the planning phase is complete, a program specification document is created and given to the software systems analyst or programmer. The goal of this diagram is to draw a high level flow of each process in the program. It also states the basic logic of the program in a step-by-step series. UML's activity diagram is a flow chart, but it includes tools to conceptualize ideas for object-oriented analysis and design. The program specifications are used to generate the activity diagram. The steps to draw an activity diagram are as follows:

1. Read the overview and scope sections of the program specifications document
2. Each item in scope should translate into one or more activities
3. Draw the activity on the diagram

Draw this diagram with certain discretion: the emphasis is high level: if the activity is "process item," do not break down the activity into "store in array" or "use malloc()." The diagram generally states the method/function/subroutine calls that are in the main routine.

Figure 1: Example Activity Diagram

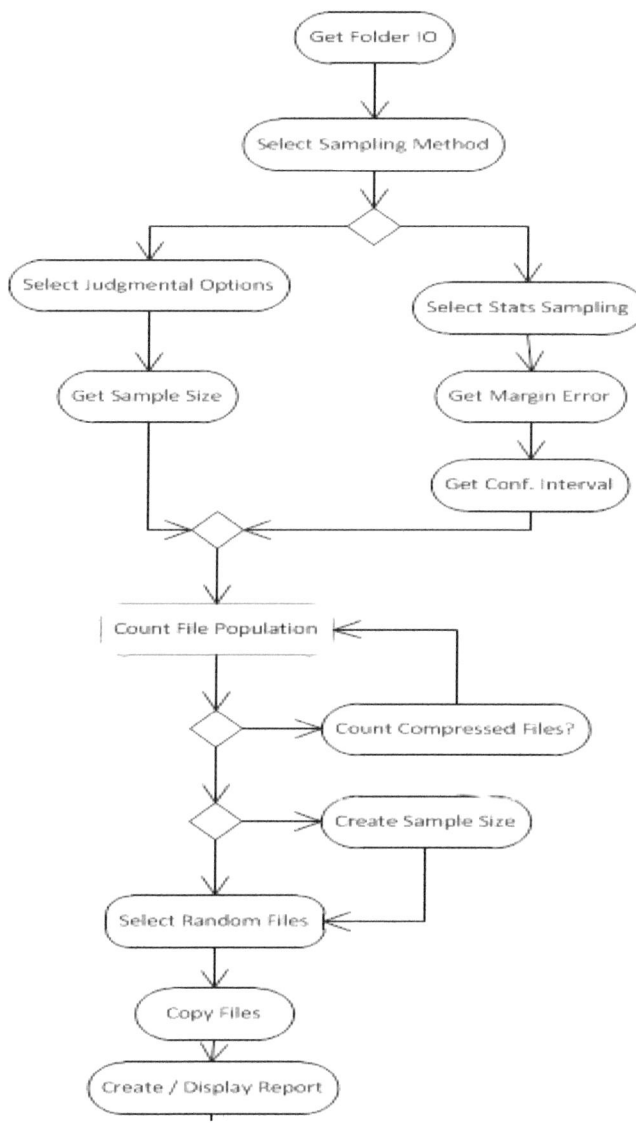

Use Case Descriptions

After the activity diagram is drawn, use case descriptions are a series of documents created using each activity from the activity diagram. Use case descriptions contain several essential things:

1. Use case name
2. ID
3. Primary actor
4. Use Case Type
5. Description
6. Relationships
7. Flow of events

The use case name is generated for each activity from the activity diagram. An ID number is more or less a page number. The primary actor is several things: an object associated with this use case, a real-life entity interacting with the program, the program interacting with a use case, or the another system interacting with a use case. Brief Description defines the activity/use case and the flow of process/activities associated with it. Relationships map inheritance relationships, required flows, optional flows, or a loose generalization relationship with something. The flow of events has normal flows which are the main processes or steps of this activity/use case. Subflows might be an alternate, branching condition associated with the specific normal flow. Each Normal flow may have none, one, or many subflows. A use case type declares either an include (required) or exclude (optional/conditional) relationship with other use cases. Drawing this relationship is essential to drawing the use case diagram.

The more time spent on the use case descriptions will make it simpler to draw the use case diagram and also the CRC cards. The use case descriptions can help with creating the CRC cards.

Figure 2: Use Case Description Example

Use Case Name:	Process Click Event		ID :	1	Importance Level:
Primary Actor:	User		Use Case Type:		Essential

Stakeholders and Interests: User- person running the program to audit documents

Brief Description: Once button clicked, the program processes the documents by taking the file population, creating a sample by selecting files, and copying the sampled files into an output directory

Trigger: User clicks button

Type: External

Relationships:

    Association: User

    Include: Select Sampling Method, Select Output Folder, Select folders for Audit

    Extend: Select NIST Filter

    Generalization:

Normal Flow of Events:

1. User clicks the Process button
2. File population is counted; a list is built of all the files
3. Calculate the sample size (using proper sample size formula)
4. Process the sample
5. Display/Save output

SubFlows:
1a. User Selects options for either Judgmental or Statistical Sampling
1b. User might select the NIST Filter option
2a. If any container files are present in the sample, extract the files and count the files from the container. Also add them to the population
2b. If NIST Filter is selected, keep a list of the hashes for the files in the population
4a. Forensically Copy files from population
Alternate/Exceptional Flows:

Use Case Diagram

The use case descriptions are used to generate this diagram. Every circle in the use case diagram represents a use case description. Each circle (the use case) is named from the use case name. Draw one of use case circles in one of the corners. Use the references section on each use case description to draw the relationships between the use cases. When all the uses cases and their associations are mapped, draw how each actor (if any) is associated with the use cases.

Blank arrows are either general relationship representing the activities are connected. An extends represents a conditional relationship and includes represents are required relationship (NOTE: MS Visio uses "uses" instead of "includes" to represent a required use case).

The emphasis on this diagram is to show how each process (use case) is associated with actors (either users or declared objects) and other processes (use cases). This diagram does show the program flow, but it is not as relevant as showing the relationships between the use cases.

There may be several disconnected sets of use cases (which there should be in most programs). These are drawn in the same box, but not connected to other set use cases.

Figure 3: Use Case Diagram Example

CRC Cards

The goal is to plan and create all the content for the classes. The analyst creating the CRC cards may refer to the previously made documents and diagrams for the methods contained in each class. Each routine will be grouped into a specific class. However, there is much more to do than grouping methods together. Each class must have attributes to hold data, a description of its purpose, and mapping of how classes are related.

The analyst must use creativity and some guess-work to the design of the classes since some of the content on CRC cards is not from previous documents and diagrams. Creating these cards may require role playing: pretend to be the class and how it interacts with other entities in the system (program). Reference the use case descriptions for how the methods function.

CRC cards (class-responsibilities-collaboration) plans the attributes and methods in each class. The cards also show the interactions between other classes and concrete objects. There is a description field for defining the class's purpose. Writing the class name is required. Responsibilities are the methods the class contains. Most CRC cards use terms for the methods such as "Get Item" not "getItem()." Attributes are the variables the class will contain. The variable type to whether it is a primitive, object, collections, etc. is written in parentheses next to the variable declarations.

Collaborators and relationships may contain the same content. For instance, there is a person interacting with part of the program, but there is also a Person class for saving the person's settings. The person interacting with the program is the collaborator. A collaborator is simply a declaration that this class will be associated with another entity. The relationships section is a detailed list of how the class is associated with other classes. The Person class is listed under relationships to show inheritance, associations, or aggregation.

> **Inheritance (is-a):** Basic OO concept; if there is a Mechanic class, a mechanic is a Person which the Mechanic inherits attributes and methods from Person. A Mechanic and Person both have a Name attribute and a walk method, but Mechanic may have a separate fix method and isGreasy method.

Aggregation (has-parts-of): This relationship represents a group, list, or collection of entities. Example: if there is a Bus class, it may contain several Tires. It's an aggregate because there is a group of parts associated with Bus. Therefore, a Bus has-parts-of Tires.

Associations: These are "loosely" related items. For example, the main Form in a program calls the Bus class for a variable declaration. It is neither an inheritance or aggregation, but listing these is not always required.

Figure 4: CRC Card Example

Class name: NSRLList	Collaborators
Responsibilities • Convert array to string • Compare Hashes • Calculate MD5 hash • Calculate SHA1 hash • Parse NSRL entry • Read NSRL Entry from file list	• frmMainForm • NSRLEntries

Description: Files can be hashed with this class. Hashes can also be compared.	**Relationships**
Attributes • File • Entry • NSRLHashList	• frmMainForm • NSRLEntries (one List has many entries)

Class Diagram

The purpose of this diagram is to take the CRC cards and draw the classes with possible associations. Some class diagrams show the relationship mappings (such as inheritance), but others simply list each class containing attributes with type, attribute access modifiers (private, public), methods, and method access modifiers (and sometimes type).

The CRC cards convert directly into this diagram. The cards show all the attributes and methods, but also map the relationships between each class. Sometimes it is important to show the relationships, but other times it is not necessary. It may be better to leave the class relationships to the coding. For example, not every program is going to have inherited classes.

When the class diagram is complete, the programmer can start coding. The programmer needs access to all the design diagrams since almost each diagram has a document that explains each entity in further detail. The class diagram gives the programmer a barebones program with all the class declarations with each having its methods and attributes. Some CASE tools generate this type of "barebones" program, but most of the coding is done by hand.

Each class contains the class name on top followed by the attributes, and then the method declarations. This is the general format from each version of UML class diagrams.

Figure 5: Example Class Diagram (without relationship mappings)

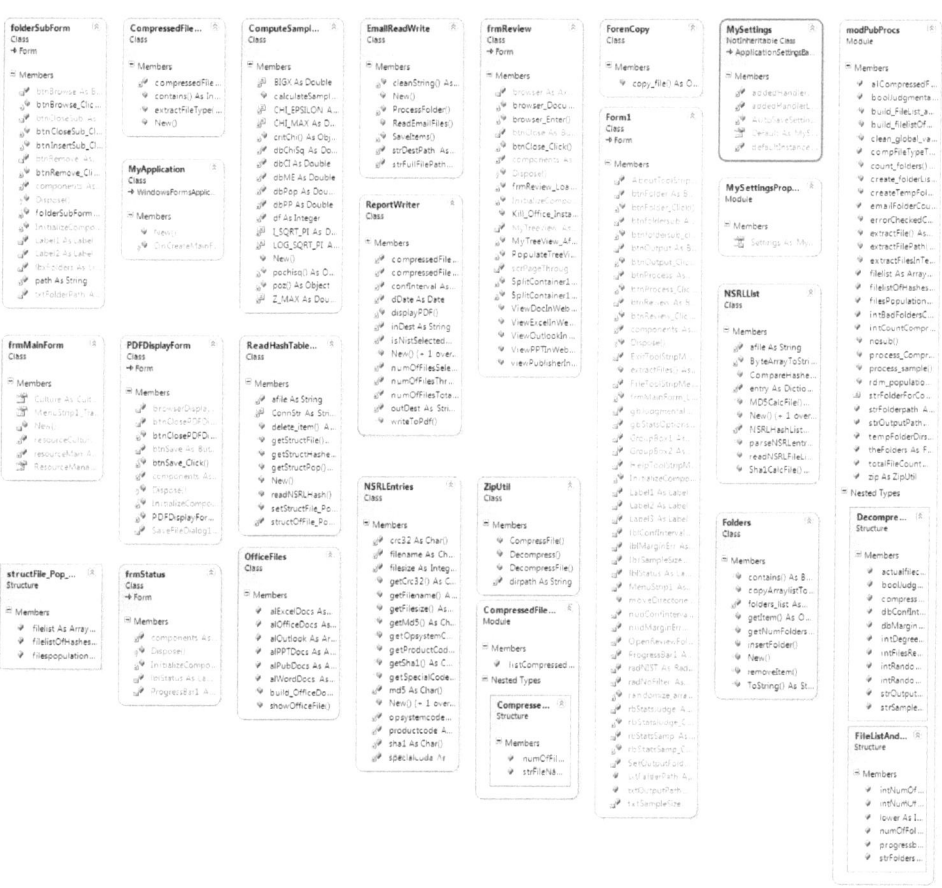

Produced with Microsoft Visual Studio 2010

Implementation

This document section explains coding, testing, prototyping, release, and maintaining. Coding refers to the programmer writing the software in the specific programming language(s). Testing involves peers validating the software operates correctly. Prototyping is either a demo or close-to-release software. Release can be a completed goal, milestone, or version release (that may have additional features in the future). Maintaining refers to fixing after development bugs and adding new features for properly operating software.

Coding

The programmer is mainly involved while others may have little involvement with coding. The specific programming language should have been chosen before or during analysis and design (if not, choose now).

Coding Tools

The programmer should be using the proper tools, such as an IDE, to develop the application. Thus, a .NET application should be developed in Visual Studio, Eclipse with Java, gcc/gdb/text editor for C in GNU/Linux, etc. Developers should decide which tools they want to use. There are several factors to consider when picking programming tools:

- Most likely, developers will user industry standard tools (Visual Studio for .NET)
- If you are unsure which tools (IDEs, editors, compilers, debuggers, etc.) are best for the language, use the internet to research the recommended tools
- If working in a team of programmers, consider using the same IDE since project files will need to be shared
- If an IDE is unavailable, use text editors such as NotePad++ or TextPad will highlight keywords, indent automatically, allow compilers/linkers add-ins, etc.
- Text editor and compiler only should be the last resort. However, most languages have developer tools: even C programming in GNU/Linux can use Eclipse as a front-end for gcc and gdb.

Documentation

Documentation includes proper comments in code and the creation of API documents. Good documentation requires a comment for at least every five code lines (on average). It also requires every class, module, source file, method declaration, etc. have comments directly before explaining the purpose of the declaration. These possibly the variable parameters and return values, if applicable.

API documents include the declarations consisting of classes, variables, methods, etc. in the program. Most IDEs use a special commenting system (different from its regular comment symbols) for the generation of API. .NET uses XML tags to generate an API XML document. Programs such as SandCastle for .NET are free to use to convert the XML files into API documents. For Java, JavaDocs is simplified, but the same idea. It is recommended to use the proper program and commenting system to generate the API documents. Check your API generator's documentation for details.

If the specific IDE does not allow API generation or no tool exists, create a copy of the CRC cards or Class Diagram and modify them to emulate an API.

Code Clarity

Code should be written for other programmers to read. Keep code legible and clean, when possible.

Testing

A software testing plan should be agreed on by the development team. The software should be reviewed by a peer. This allows overlooked bugs to become uncovered and possible suggestions (such as a logical layout to the user interface). The bugs should be discussed with the development team.

Software testing generally does not include debugging through an IDE such as Visual Studio or Eclipse. The programmer should use a debugger while developing code. However, some debuggers can uncover security flaws in the code (i.e. gdb can analyze the stack frame if a buffer overflow occurs). If the development team feels the need to require additional debugging sessions separate from programming to assure quality, than it should be included.

Prototype

A prototype is not the finished program, but is an unfinished and small-scale version of the program used for testing purposes. Testers will use the prototype during the testing phase. When testers use the prototype, they should be aware it is not a finished piece of software.

Release

When the software requirements and bug fixes are complete, the program can be released. A program specification document (or requirements document) was created in the planning phase. This document should define the deliverables and expectations of the final release.

NOTE: A release is the latest stable version. The program was thoroughly debugged and tested at a stable release.

Any "last minute" features that are not in the program specification document should not be implemented. Refer to the maintenance phase for "last minute" features.

Maintenance

The goal of maintenance is continuous improvement: as bugs are found or features are requested, the software is updated.

After the release of a program, code needs updating. Sometimes users want additional features or a bug is discovered which was not found in testing or development. The ideal program is bug free, but a good program has minimal bugs in reality.

Reporting bugs should be done in a systematic way. Contact the development team to report a bug.

Discussing and agreeing upon new features is important. The developers need an objective to obtain: new features may require iterating through the development cycle, but if it is a small feature, it may not be necessary. The program specification document should be updated to track these changes. Within in the updates made on the program specification document, it should be noted the program is in the maintenance phase and list the new features to be implemented.

Appendix I: Key Terms

Analysis and Design: Software development cycles usually have planning, analysis, design, implementation, etc. Analysis and Design is used synonymously with Object-Oriented Analysis and Design

Application Programming Interface (API): An API is a software component that allows other software components to communicate with one another.

CASE tools: Computer Aided Software Engineering tools; software used for drawing program design diagrams (mostly UML diagrams)

Class Responsibility Collaboration (CRC) cards: CRC cards are used to design classes in OOAD. CRC in this document is not to be confused with cyclical redundancy checks

Integrated Development Environment (IDE): An IDE is an application that assists programmers with developing software. The IDE includes a compiler, interpreter and a place for organizing code and validating code syntax.

Object Oriented (OO): Object oriented programming is a method using classes and inheritance to efficiently organize software code. Objects can process data or send and receive messages. A process is contained in an object and then that object is used or "called" whenever that process is needed by the program.

Software Development: This does not only contain programming, but includes other steps such as project approval, requirements gathering, drawing design diagrams, etc.

Subroutine/function/method: Language dependent term for a process-oriented part of the program.

UML: Unified Modeling Language; standard design diagrams and documents used in object-oriented analysis and design; a consortia of major software development companies and academics created these standards for UML.